MOON FRUIT

MOON FRUIT
nourishment in the midst of hardship

Morgan Bullock

Copyright © 2018 by Morgan Bullock
All rights reserved. This book or any portion thereof may not be reproduced or used in any manner whatsoever without the express written permission of the publisher except for the use of brief quotations in a book review.

Cover artwork by Nico Pendleton

ISBN: 0578412640
ISBN-13: 978-0578412641

In Memory of my brother, Jacob, whose light and love touched many.

To my son, Malakhi, a flower who blooms in God's garden and in my heart forever.

For You, in hopes that you will grow in light, love, peace and joy.

This book is incomplete... without you. I have left the backsides of every page blank waiting for you to complete them. Complete them with your art, with your reactions, with your anger or with your tears. Complete them with your journey to becoming Moon Fruit. I hope that you write about your feelings and let out your fears. I want you to rip out the pages that resonate with you the most and hang them on your wall or in a frame or fold them up and put them in your pocket or your wallet. I am planting a seed within and watering you with my words. Go, grow and be fruitful.

I believe in you.

Love always,

Morgan

Morgan Bullock

what is?

Moon fruit needs no water oxygen or things from this world. Only through the light of the Son is it able to grow and ultimately feed others.

Moon fruit grows in the midst of darkness, against all odds and contrary to popular belief. Moon fruit doesn't grow for its own self victory but to nourish others growing through darkness.

MOON FRUIT

IN BETWEEN

I want the world to love me for who I am.

I tell the world to be patient with me while I grow.

BUT...

I don't do that for myself.

I don't allow myself to just be.

I am not patient with my personal journey.

I am in constant desire to be at my fabricated destination.

How can I require something from the world that I do not practice myself?

allow yourself to be.

MOON FRUIT

Morgan Bullock

Real Love

To love yourself is a choice you have to make daily.

> Loving your self does not end with your attributes it includes your flaws, misfortunes and poor decisions.

MOON FRUIT

It's okay to cry,
I don't wipe my tears. Instead I let them fall into puddles on my pillow so when I stop I can see the pain I have released.

It's okay to cry,
I often times cry in the mirror to observe myself in my most vulnerable state. I admire the sight of pain and strength interlarded within me.

It's okay to cry,
I will cry until my eyes puff, my head hurts and my body aches. I will scream to the top of my lungs in mourning.

It's okay to cry,
I cry myself to sleep.

MOON FRUIT

SHOWERS

I learned to only cry in the shower. So my tears would be disguised by the hot water beating upon my face. So I could have an excuse for my red face and puffy eyes. So my sobs could be drowned out by the wringing out of my wash rag... all I wished was for my sorrows to be washed down the drain with each wring. I would stand there and cry until my eyes dried up and the steam vanished. All I wished was for my pain to vanish with it.

MOON FRUIT

Morgan Bullock

Joy Comes in the Morning

Past midnight pain consumes me.

By sunrise peace is overwhelming

MOON FRUIT

> "Remember, a rose that blossoms through concrete possess more beauty than a dozen roses that bloom in a garden"
>
> \- An Old Friend

I'm stuck between a rock and a harder rock. I find cement blocks on my feet. Fear on my left and fragility on my right keeping me below the surface with the weight of my grief on my shoulders. The only outlet is up through my vulnerability and strength that lies deep within. It's a journey in itself to travel that deep inside my soul. But it's a journey I must take for the only way to grow and blossom from these two hard rocks and cement blocks is to be deeply rooted in who I am and the person I am meant to be. Freedom is on the other side of this world filled with concrete. Fight fear. Accept your fragility. Show your vulnerability.

B L O O M.

MOON FRUIT

Morgan Bullock

|tidal.

                      I am in control of the tides in my life.

I let the waves of my troubles ravish against my feet and rise above my shoulders.

    I retreat when my soul gets weary.

        I ask God to wash away my sins

            and my sorrow.

           Then

I task him with the same request the night after.

I am the moon of my universe.

    I can illuminate the sky

        or hide behind the clouds.

MOON FRUIT

Jacob

No matter how much I try I can't disguise my puffy eyes, this pounding headache, these tears from falling, this broken heart from missing you.

It's been almost a decade since I've lost you but it feels like a life time.

I'm known by many as the strong friend, the one who handles the unimaginable with poise and grace and a smile on her face. But beneath it all she is broken, hurt and unsure as to why it all seems to happen to her.

Wounds heal but you are left with scars.

Scars hurt when it rains or when it's cold outside or randomly with no explanation.

It is as though I'm walking around with one leg or without my thumbs. I've learned how to make it work but they are still gone and boy do I miss the ease of grasping anything I please without thinking twice. It's like developing a peanut allergy at 22 after you've fallen in love with peanut butter and jelly sandwiches. And it doesn't stop anyone from eating them right in front of your face.

MOON FRUIT

Jacob Cont.

"Time heals all wounds"

They don't talk about the scars though.

You were like my thumbs or my big toes, not a defining part of me but once gone the simplest of tasks became difficult and I became unbalanced.

While I've learned to manage, it took me years to realize, after you were amputated from my life, that you, like limbs, would not grow back and the phantom limb pain would not subside.

MOON FRUIT

We look for others who understand our feelings and emotions. We long for a friend in times of need.

As they say – whoever 'they' are – "misery loves company"

I like to think misery loves company in hopes of encouragement.

Find solace in knowing that you are not alone for in fact we all go through.

MOON FRUIT

Loveship

Friends are friends until true friendship is required. Strive for loveship because love, well... love never fails.

Loveship is allowing your heart to pour out to others accepting them as they are; interlarding your circles, feeding their souls and dancing with their spirits at the cadence of your heartbeat. Do not hoard this love for your significant other. Moon Fruit does not grow to only feed one soul, Moon Fruit feeds many but only few will find themselves worthy.

MOON FRUIT

It is a peculiar thing when the world in fact stops but you are the only one who notices. It is perplexing to watch others carry on cluelessly as though they did not just feel what happened. The magnitude of your situation is minuet to everyone but you. It is insulting, somewhat crippling, shifting you back to that place of numbness. The fog from this confusion leaves your mind stagnate.
In in the midst of it all don't forget to proceed.

MOON FRUIT

Morgan Bullock

GO FORTH

AHEAD

CONTINUE

RESUME

MOVE FORWARD

ADVANCE

PROGRESS

MARCH ON

PROCEED

MOON FRUIT

RIVERS OF LIVING WATER

Moon Fruit can withstand a drought of any kind.

It drinks from rivers, creeks and streams of living water that flows within those who follow the Son of God.

To withstand the plagues of this earth you must uphold a truth much greater than this world.

He will quench your thirst for a lifetime.

MOON FRUIT

Morgan Bullock

In times of dark days and moonlit paths, shoulders become a familiar place. They subconsciously turn into reservoirs filled with your tears.
To have one is a blessing
Two is more than enough.

Remember to allow others to water your shoulders too. For we all have rainy days.

Shoulders

MOON FRUIT

Don't be afraid to go through some shit. Name someone who has made a positive impact on the world who didn't have to go through some shit.

Greatness doesn't come from people who don't have to go through some shit. Perfect picket fenced happy ass lives rarely give anything back to the world. Tests, trials and tribulations produce fruit.

Shit seems to be filled with the nutrients we need to grow. Let the shit you go through fertilize your soul. Without fertilizer how will you bear fruit? The shit you get is a blessing. Thank God He believes in your greatness.

Don't sit in your shit. Take what you can from it and build.

Your shit is a blessing far from a curse.

MOON FRUIT

Morgan Bullock

Fertilizer,
Made of your
Misfortunes
Tribulations
& Losses.
Nourishment
for the soul
Strength for the heart.

MOON FRUIT

Sun showers and moon cries are a part of it all. Take notice when the rain doesn't drown out the light.

And when there are too many clouds and the rain forms puddles that grow into floods keep in mind that the moon doesn't stay hidden. In most cases she comes out tomorrow.

Don't hate the cloudy days; they reminds us of how much we need the light.

MOON FRUIT

The silence is deafening. I scream to the top of my lungs at the highest octave my voice can achieve releasing the pain deep within. I hear the shrieks and cracks in my voice indicating my humanness only for it all to be drowned by the ever present silence.

Silence swallows the everyday sounds; the voice of your lover, the chirp of the birds in the morning.

Silence reminds you that you are in fact alone.

MOON FRUIT

Morgan Bullock

Just when I thought it was getting better.
The moment I thought my tears were dried up.
The weight of the world found it's resting place
upon my shoulders again.

•

I assumed that weight had left. I shooed it away
only to realize it was continuing to fatigue my
heart and put a toll on my soul.

MOON FRUIT

Don't rush your journey. Peeling green bananas does not ripen them faster. It leaves you with bitter fruit.

MOON FRUIT

Life is not a race. Flowers are not praised for blooming first. Fruit is not enjoyed for being harvested first. It is the brightest flower and the sweetest fruit that make the difference. Those things, like you, take time.

MOON FRUIT

Morgan Bullock

THE NOTION THAT YOU ARE NOT GOOD ENOUGH IS A LIE YOU HAVE ACCEPTED AND DIGESTED AS THE TRUTH IT IS UP TO YOU TO REGURGITATE AND DISPEL WHAT YOU HAVE BELIEVED FOR SO LONG

MOON FRUIT

Your moonlight only shines as bright as you let it. It only goes as far as you allow it.

The world is only as small as you make it.

MOON FRUIT

Nothing will happen overnight.

Success, happiness and love take time.

Healing takes time.

Eventually though, your breakthrough will be tomorrow.

Soon enough your tomorrow will be today.

MOON FRUIT

Morgan Bullock

Our thoughts determine everything.

Choose to think of the positive
Decide to think of your ups.
Find your light and focus on it.

MOON FRUIT

Don't Run

Do not run from your pain. Do not subscribe to the notion that strength is found in not giving a fuck or never allowing yourself to be phased by anything.

Strength is found in acknowledging your pain, obstacle, bump in the road and enduring/growing from it and through it.

Ignoring pain spirals you into remaining immature and stunts your growth.

MOON FRUIT

Morgan Bullock

Pain is Universal

The feeling of your heart gaining a pound.

The lump in your throat clogging your air way

The tears welling up reaching the brim of your eyelids waiting to fall the moment you break your gaze

The numbness that takes over your body making you question your reality

The emptiness you feel after realizing it was not a dream.

The screaming to the top of your lungs only to be heard by no one at all.

The aching of your muscles after constantly weeping

The gasping for air thanks to your mind forcing you to breath when in your heart you'd rather hold your breath for eternity.

MOON FRUIT

Pain is Universal Cont.

We may love differently. Our preferences may be opposite. Our thoughts may clash. Our ideas could be on the opposite ends of the spectrum. Our walk, talk, humor and frustration could all ride a different wave length. Our situation, location, beliefs and morals may all be like oil and water.

But our pain...

Pain is universal we all know what hurt feels like. We know the struggle of trying to see in the midst of darkness. Someone across the seven seas relates to me with pain...

As well as with joy.

Joy is Universal

MOON FRUIT

Joy

Strive for joy.

Joy is found deep within given to you by God. Whatever your circumstance, joy never fades.

Happiness comes and goes and changes with the weather but joy. Joy is as constant as the sun rising in the morning and the moon coming out to play in the evening.

MOON FRUIT

Morgan Bullock

Everything happens for a reason.

Sometimes the reason has nothing to do with you.

MOON FRUIT

Have you experienced the feeling of sadness due to thinking about the sadness someone feels for you? The feeling of knowing your loved one sees your tragedy and their heart breaks for you. Their heart break causes your heart break creating a cycle of heart break until you both piece each other back together.

I think of my
lover
father
mother

My heart broke knowing that they knew they couldn't do anything to mend mine.

Still... let others be strong for you.

MOON FRUIT

Morgan Bullock

It is after the rain
when I can truly
smell the flowers

It is after the pain
when I can truly
start to bloom

MOON FRUIT

Can you die
from a broken heart?

I hold on to people
and things
and places
and moments
as though losing them
will kill me.

Let go

MOON FRUIT

Don't be the caterpillar afraid to cocoon while watching others turn into butterflies.

For the pain of transforming yields great beauty.

MOON FRUIT

Unhealthy

I'll let you peek through the window allowing you to assume I have it all together

but I wouldn't dare open the door to let you see me from the inside.

MOON FRUIT

Morgan Bullock

How is it that I can be content and excited about my position in life yet also mourn the excitement I once had?

MOON FRUIT

Duality

I am learning the complexities of my heart.
How she can be overjoyed and in great mourning
simultaneously.

MOON FRUIT

When you are rendered speechless

Lean on your heart for the words

Let your soul speak for a change

MOON FRUIT

Morgan Bullock

Know this,
With everything, or nothing at all
You are somebody.

MOON FRUIT

Negative thoughts always knock first.
You choose to let them in.

MOON FRUIT

Morgan Bullock

I didn't notice
funeral homes
until we had to use one.
I didn't understand death
until we lost you.

I didn't notice
my uniqueness
until you showed me how much you liked it
I didn't know love
until I found you.

I didn't notice
how colorful the world was
until you gave me joy
I didn't know faith
until You found me.

I Was Blind But Now I See

MOON FRUIT

When you are running out of energy and your breath is short.
When you wonder if you can make it to the end or if you should give up...

Remember, God equipped you with a second wind
and winners don't walk through
the finish line.

Push through

- Endurance

MOON FRUIT

Why do you cry over rainy days
as if the sun won't come out tomorrow?
Is your faith only strong when the sun is shining?

MOON FRUIT

Morgan Bullock

Lord I love you.
I love what you do inside of me.
I thank you for these tears
these emotions
...
Because without them
who would I be?

MOON FRUIT

Morgan Bullock

no one
owes you

you owe it
to yourself

MOON FRUIT

Morgan Bullock

I BRUSH GOD OFF
AND
THROW HIM TO
THE SIDE
AS THOUGH HE IS
NOT... GOD

THEN I WONDER
WHY I'M
MET WITH
MOUNTAINS
MADE UP OF MY
DOUBTS
FEARS AND
INSECURITIES

MOON FRUIT

ONLY WITH GOD CAN MOUNTAINS BE MOVED.

ONLY GOD WILL HE KEEP THEM OUT OF MY WAY.

MOON FRUIT

Morgan Bullock

Just as sure as you are
about the sun rising
and rainy days in April,

be just as sure of yourself.

MOON FRUIT

About the Author

Morgan Bullock has a BFA in Creative Writing from Florida State University where she was a student athlete on the Seminole Softball team. During her athletic career, Morgan was the Editor-in-Chief of the Seminole Softball newsletter and had a blog spot on Seminoles.com. Her writing is inspired by the emotional healing, personal growth and the journey to finding self-worth. She is an Atlanta native where she currently resides. Morgan enjoys deep car conversations with old and new friends and seeks the good in everyone and everything.